LEGENDS OF WOMEN'S FIGURE SKATING

Maura Sullivan Hill

Abbeville Kids
An Imprint of Abbeville Press
New York London

Statistics are current as of July 8, 2025.

Project editor: Lauren Orthey
Copy editor: Jennifer Dixon
Designer: Ada Rodriguez
Production director: Louise Kurtz

PHOTOGRAPHY CREDITS

Adobe Stock: front cover background (Rawpixel.com); pp. 2–3 (StockVideoFactory); pp. 4–5 (Damerfie), pp. 62–63 background (Smile)

Alamy: front cover left (speedpix), front cover center (Ulrik Pedersen/NurPhoto), front cover right (PCN Photography/PCN Black), p. 7 (KEYSTONE Pictures USA/ZUMA Press), p. 9 and back cover top (PCN Photography), p. 11 and back cover bottom (Christophe Guibbaud/Cameleon/ABACAPRESS), p. 13 (Johnny Syversen/NTB), p. 15 (PCN Photography/PCN Black), p. 19 (Keystone Press/KEYSTONE Pictures USA), p. 23 (Serena S.Y. Hsu/ZUMA Press), p. 25 (PCN Photography/PCN Black), p. 27 and back cover center (Hy Peskin/Alon Alexander), p. 29 (Classic Picture Library), p. 31 (PA Images), p. 33 (PCN Photography/PCN Black), p. 35 (PCN Photography/PCN Black), p. 37 (PCN Photography/PCN Black), p. 39 (PCN Photography/PCN Black), p. 41 (Amanda Sabga/UPI/Alamy Live News), p. 45 (PCN Photography/PCN Black), p. 49 (Raniero Corbelletti/Aflo Co. Ltd./Nippon News/Alamy Live News), p. 51 (Tony Marshall/PA Images), p. 55 (Paul Sutton-PCN/PCN Photography), p. 59 (PCN Photography/PCN Black), p. 61 (PCN Photography/PCN Black), p. 63 (PCN Photography/PCN Black)

Imago: p. 21 (Sven Simon), p. 43 (Anders Wiklund/TT), p. 47 (Werek), p. 57 (TT)

Mabel Fairbanks Estate: p. 17 (photo courtesy of the estate of Mabel Fairbanks)

Wikimedia Commons: p. 53 (*The Art of Skating*, Irving Brokaw/American Sports)

First edition
10 9 8 7 6 5 4 3 2 1

Library of Congress Cataloging-in-Publication Data available upon request

For bulk and premium sales and for text adoption procedures, write to Customer Service Manager, Abbeville Press, 655 Third Avenue, New York, NY 10017, or call 1-800-ARTBOOK.

Visit Abbeville Kids online at www.abbevillefamily.com.

CONTENTS

Tenley Albright

Tenley Albright made history on the ice and then became a trailblazer for women in the medical field. Not only was she the first American woman to win the World Championships and the Olympic Games in women's figure skating, but Tenley was one of just five women in her graduating class from Harvard Medical School.

So how did she do it? With the inspiration of her own often-quoted motto: "If you are not falling down, you're not trying something that is hard enough." Tenley adds, "You learn disappointment comes with trying to be your best, and that's a valuable life lesson."

It all started on a backyard skating rink in Newton, Massachusetts. Tenley's father, a successful surgeon, built the rink for Tenley, a figure skater, and her brother, Niles, a speed skater. She loved jumping on the ice and the feeling of flying that came with it, until she was hospitalized with polio at the age of 10. Tenley lost the use of her legs, back, and neck, and some doctors thought she might never walk again. But with what would become her trademark persistence, Tenley not only walked again, but got back on the ice and performed at a competition just four months after coming home from the hospital.

At age 15, she competed at the senior level for the first time, earning a silver medal at the US Championships in 1951. From then on, Tenley dominated at the US Championships, winning the gold medal from 1952 to 1956. After a surprise silver medal at the 1952 Olympics in Oslo, Norway, Tenley won her first World Championship the next year in 1953, the first by an American woman. She took silver at Worlds in 1954, then earned the gold medal again the following year in 1955, becoming the first woman in the sport to lose and regain a World title.

Tenley was the favorite heading into the 1956 Olympics in Cortina, Italy, but disaster struck when she injured her ankle two weeks before the competition. Once again displaying her determination, she competed and won the gold medal, another first for an American woman.

During the height of her skating career, Tenley was also a student at Radcliffe College, a women's college in Cambridge, Massachusetts, that is now part of Harvard University. She woke up at 4 AM to practice on the ice before a full day of classes at Radcliffe, then returned to the rink after school for more skating. Even though she was offered a contract to skate with the Ice Capades touring ice show after her Olympic victory, Tenley decided to pursue medical school at Harvard, following in her father's footsteps to a successful surgical career. She practiced medicine for more than 20 years, taught at Harvard Medical School, and worked on international initiatives to eradicate polio, her childhood disease.

Birthdate: July 18, 1935
Hometown: Newton Centre, Massachusetts
Country Represented: USA

Olympics
Appearances: 1952, 1956
S 1952 G 1956

World Championships
Appearances: 1951, 1953–56
G 1953, 1955 S 1954, 1956

National Championships
Appearances: 1951–56
S 1951 G 1952–56

Mao Asada

You can't talk about Mao Asada without talking about the triple axel. It's the only jump with a forward takeoff followed by three and a half rotations in the air, and it's one of the most difficult jumps ever performed in women's skating. It was Mao's go-to move. She was an incredible jumper, even as a young junior skater, competing at the level right below the Olympic level. In 2005, she was the first female skater to land a triple axel at the World Junior Championships. And when she made it to the Olympics, in 2010, she became the first woman to land three triple axels in one competition, one in the short program and two in the free skate.

Japanese women's skaters have a long history with the triple axel. Midori Ito was the first woman to land the jump in competition, in 1988. Midori's coach, Machiko Yamada, coached Mao and her sister, Mai, who also competed internationally for Japan. When Mao first skated at the Japan Figure Skating Championships, at age 12, she wore one of Midori's old costumes and jumped a triple axel of her own.

Mao had a lot of success at a young age. She won the Grand Prix Final at the senior level in 2006, when she was 15–too young to compete at the 2006 Olympics in Turin, Italy, just a few months later. The age rules at the time were different for the Olympics than other skating competitions, and many skating fans and experts thought it was unfair that she couldn't compete, when she was one of the best in the world.

The next year, 2007, Mao won the first of her five World Championship medals, a silver. She won medals at the Four Continents Championships and the Grand Prix Final six times over the course of her career, plus three World Championships gold medals.

Mao often competed against South Korea's Yuna Kim, and their rivalry on the ice was exciting to watch. At the 2010 Olympics in Vancouver, Canada, Mao finished second to Yuna, even with those three triple axels, but she continued competing, driven by dreams of the 2014 Olympics in Sochi, Russia.

The triple axel that had been Mao's trademark throughout her career was her downfall in Sochi. She fell on the triple axel in the short program and ended up in 16th place after that portion of the competition. There would be no chance for a second Olympic medal, but her near-perfect performance in the free skate, with two triple axels, showed her strength and won the hearts of skating fans everywhere. After finishing sixth at the Olympics, Mao went on to win her third World title on home ice in Japan, then embarked on a show-skating career. She attempted a comeback ahead of the 2018 Olympics, but ultimately decided to focus on skating in shows.

In 2024, a rink named after Mao opened in Tokyo, and she announced her plans to coach skaters at the facility, ready to inspire the next generation as Midori Ito had inspired her.

Birthdate: September 25, 1990
Hometown: Nagoya, Japan
Country Represented: Japan

Olympics
Appearances: 2010, 2014
S 2010

World Championships
Appearances: 2007–14, 2016
G 2008, 2010, 2014
S 2007
B 2013

National Championships
Appearances: 2003–14, 2016–17
G 2007–10, 2012–13
S 2005–6, 2011
B 2014, 2016

Surya Bonaly

By age 10, Surya Bonaly knew that she loved how it felt when she jumped across the ice as a figure skater–it was like flying. So it's no surprise that she is most remembered for taking flight. Surya is the first and only skater to land a backflip on one skate at the Olympic Games.

A backflip is more common in gymnastics than on the ice, and Surya started out in gymnastics as a kid growing up in Nice, by the ocean in the south of France. She was adopted at 18 months old by Suzanne and Georges Bonaly. They gave her the name Surya, which means "sun" in Sanskrit, an ancient Indian language. The family lived a very simple lifestyle on a farm. When Surya wanted to watch the televised figure skating events during the 1984 Olympics, they had to save up electricity from the solar panels to run the TV.

Surya was active in many sports as a child, in part because her mom was a gym teacher. She did gymnastics, trampoline, and skating, but skating was her favorite sport. Her coach was a French national champion, which made Surya want to win a national title of her own. And she did, not just once but nine times in a row, from 1989 to 1997.

Surya was a strong jumper with an athletic style of skating, known for landing combinations with multiple triple jumps. She won the European Championships five times in a row, from 1991 to 1995.

Despite these achievements, Surya also experienced prejudice in her skating career because of the color of her skin. She did not hesitate to speak out when she thought things were unfair, as when she finished in second place at the 1994 World Championships in a close decision by the judges. She declined to wear her medal in protest of the results. "I wanted the judges to know I thought the scores weren't right," she later explained.

Surya competed in the Olympics three times and made history during her last appearance, in 1998 in Nagano, Japan. She was in sixth place after the short program, suffering from an Achilles tendon injury, and felt she did not have a chance at a medal. In the long program, Surya decided to forget about the judges, have fun, and make history. She spontaneously performed a backflip, with her trademark split position and one-foot landing. She had been doing the move since she was 12, but only in ice shows because it was banned in competition for safety reasons. She lost points in her final score because of the illegal backflip, but it was more important to her to leave a unique mark on the sport.

After retiring from competition, Surya performed in ice shows, doing her famous backflip until she was 40 years old. She now works as a figure skating coach.

Birthdate: December 15, 1973
Hometown: Nice, France
Country Represented: France

Olympics
Appearances: 1992, 1994, 1998

World Championships
Appearances: 1989–96
S 1993–95

National Championships
Appearances: 1989–98
G 1989–97
S 1998

Lu Chen

Lu Chen grew up in Northeast China and was the daughter of athletes. Her mom competed in table tennis, and her dad, a former captain on the national ice hockey team, later managed the rink where Lu practiced. Lu first stepped on the ice with her dad at age four, first on a patch of ice in their yard and then at a nearby outdoor rink. She was inspired by 1968 Olympic champion Peggy Fleming after watching a TV documentary about the American skater.

Lu started skating in the 1980s, around the same time Chinese skaters first competed in international events. There weren't even any indoor rinks in the country yet, but even without ideal training conditions, Lu had success. She became the first women's skater from China to win medals at the Olympics and World Championships.

It all started in 1991, with a bronze medal at the World Junior Championships, the level below the Olympic level. Already a national champion at home in China, Lu competed at both the World Junior Championships and the World Championships that year. Sometimes skaters compete at events at both the junior and senior levels early in their senior career, as they gain competitive experience. That experience paid off for Lu when she qualified for her first Olympics, the 1992 Games in Albertville, France, where she finished sixth. That same year, she surprised everyone with a bronze medal at the World Championships, the first World medal for China.

For the next few years, Lu was usually the skater on the third step of the podium at major competitions. She won another bronze at Worlds in 1993, then followed that up with bronze at her second Olympic Games, in Lillehammer, Norway, in 1994. It was the first Olympic figure skating medal for China.

In 1995, it was not bronze but gold for Lu when she won the World Championships–yet another first for a Chinese skater.

By this point in her career, Lu had a reputation as a beautiful, expressive skater. When she set out to defend her World title in 1996, Lu was up against American Michelle Kwan. Lu skated first and delivered an elegant, artistic program. When Michelle performed, not only was she artistic, but she also added a spontaneous, extra jump at the end of her routine. The judges gave her the gold and Lu settled for silver. The next season, Lu failed to qualify for the free skate at the 1997 World Championships. Only the top 24 skaters after the short program get to compete in the free skate, and Lu had finished 25th. But she came back strong the next year, winning another bronze at the 1998 Olympics in Nagano, Japan, skating to a piece of Chinese classical music, *The Butterfly Lovers Violin Concerto*.

After the Olympics, Lu toured the US with the Stars on Ice show and then became a coach. She and her husband, 1992 Olympic pairs silver medalist Denis Petrov, have two children and coach skating together in China.

Birthdate: November 24, 1976
Hometown: Changchun, China
Country Represented: China

Olympics
Appearances: 1992, 1994, 1998
B 1994, 1998

World Championships
Appearances: 1991–93, 1995–97
G 1995
S 1996
B 1992–93

National Championships
Appearances: 1989–98
G 1989–98

Sasha Cohen

Sasha Cohen is an Olympic and World medalist in figure skating, but what set her apart most was the flexibility and elegance she displayed on the ice. Her longtime coach, John Nicks, once said: "She is unable to get into an ugly position." Whether she was spinning with her foot above her head or extending her leg in the air in a spiral, Sasha's positions combined the grace of ballet and the flexibility of gymnastics. This makes sense, since her mother, Galina, studied ballet, and Sasha started out in gymnastics before she found figure skating.

Sasha first tried skating at age seven, when she went to the rink with a friend. She immediately loved to skate fast, and that's how she met Coach Nicks, who noticed that she was the fastest skater on the ice. He became her coach through the 2002 Olympics, and then again later in her career.

Sasha—which is a Ukrainian nickname for her full name, Alexandra—was a promising young skater on the US skating scene in the late 1990s. She worked on the flexibility that became her trademark by starting and ending every day with a stretching routine. Sasha spent hours on the ice every day, so she was homeschooled from seventh grade through high school graduation.

Sasha's breakout moment was at the 2000 US Championships. She finished in second place when she was 15, which at that time was too young to go on to the World Championships. The next season, she had a back injury and could not compete, but fought to make a comeback for the Olympic season in 2002. With a silver medal at the 2002 US Championships, Sasha earned a spot at the Olympics in Salt Lake City, Utah, where she came in fourth.

Silver medals at the World Championships in 2004 and 2005 made Sasha a medal favorite heading into the next Olympics, in 2006 in Turin, Italy. She won her first US Championship that year, after years of finishing behind Michelle Kwan, a nine-time US champion. At the Olympics the following month, Sasha took the lead after the short program but then had to fight back after falling on the first two jumps in her free skate. She finished the rest of the program strong, despite an injury she had been dealing with all year, and ended up with the silver medal.

After her second Olympics, Sasha took a break from skating and trained in acting, appearing in movies and TV shows, before making a comeback in the hopes of qualifying for the 2010 Olympics. She just missed the team by placing fourth at the US Championships. Sasha performed in ice shows like Stars on Ice before attending college at Columbia University. Now working in the business world, Sasha also spends time writing, podcasting, and making TV appearances to advocate for support for elite athletes as they transition out of sports. She and her husband, Geoffrey Lieberthal, have two children.

Birthdate: October 26, 1984
Hometown: Laguna Niguel, California
Country Represented: USA

Olympics

Appearances: 2002, 2006

S 2006

World Championships

Appearances: 2002–6

S 2004–5 B 2006

National Championships

Appearances: 2000, 2002–6, 2010

G 2006 S 2000, 2002, 2004–5

B 2003 P 2010

Mabel Fairbanks

Mabel Fairbanks never won a medal in a skating competition, but it wasn't because she didn't have talent. Mabel was a skater in New York City in the 1930s, when racial segregation kept her out of rinks and competitions. She wasn't allowed to compete because she was Black. But Mabel loved to skate and had a determined personality, so she decided to make her mark on the sport in a different way, first as an ice show performer and then as a coach who empowered her fellow Black skaters.

When Mabel was a young girl, she loved to watch skaters twirl and glide on the rink in Central Park. Then she went to a theater to see the movie *One in a Million*, starring three-time Olympic champion Sonja Henie, and decided she wanted to learn to skate herself. She found a pair of used skates at a secondhand shop. They were a little big, but Mabel didn't let that hold her back. She took the skates to a frozen pond in Harlem and taught herself to glide on the ice.

But when Mabel tried to skate at rink facilities, she was turned away because of the color of her skin. Eventually, one rink owner admired her persistence and let her in to practice. It was there that a coach named Maribel Vinson Owen, a nine-time US champion, noticed her talent and gave her lessons. When Mabel wasn't allowed to compete or perform in shows, Maribel encouraged her to start her own show.

With help from a friend, Mabel figured out a way to use dry ice and water to create a small, portable ice surface, and she took it with her to venues around Harlem to perform. Then she moved to Los Angeles, California, and got a job on a TV variety show on ice, called *Frosty Frolics*. She also started coaching skating, teaching the children of many Hollywood stars. But Mabel never forgot how difficult it was for her to learn to skate as a young Black girl. She coached children of all races, but was especially determined to help other skaters of color succeed.

Mabel coached Atoy Wilson, the first Black skater to compete at the US Championships. In 1966, Atoy became the first Black skater to win a national title, at the novice level, two levels below Olympic level. She was the first coach of Tai Babilonia, who is Black, Filipino, and Hopi Indian, and Tai's pairs partner Randy Gardner, a duo that went on to win the 1979 World Championships. Mabel also mentored 1988 Olympic bronze medalist Debi Thomas, the first Black athlete to medal at the Winter Olympics.

In recognition of her impact, Mabel became the first Black woman ever inducted into the US Figure Skating Hall of Fame, in 1997. Today, there is a scholarship fund named after Mabel for skaters who are Black, Indigenous, or People of Color. Even though she passed away in 2001, Mabel's legacy continues to increase diversity in figure skating.

Birthdate: November 14, 1917
Hometown: New York, New York
Country Represented: USA

Peggy Fleming

Olympic champion Peggy Fleming is figure skating's first true TV star. She won a gold medal at the 1968 Olympics, the first Winter Olympics televised in color. The bright green skating dress (handmade by her mother) that she wore during her performance became iconic in the skating world, since viewers could see its vibrant color on their screens.

After the Olympics, Peggy starred in the first TV figure skating shows, then became the voice of American skating as a television commentator for almost three decades.

It was quite the journey for the skater from the Bay Area in California, who grew up on a farm with three sisters. As a girl, Peggy loved being outside, climbing trees, and playing baseball. But after her dad took the sisters skating one Saturday afternoon when she was nine years old, Peggy found her new favorite activity. She started skating every day that first year, and when her family moved from the farm to Pasadena, Peggy started training seriously and competing.

Her rise to the top of American skating came in the aftermath of tragedy. In 1961, the entire US team for the World Figure Skating Championships was killed in a plane crash on the way to the competition. Peggy was just 12 years old, and her coach was among those who died on the flight. In the aftermath of the tragedy, European coaches came to the US to help teach American skaters, and Peggy's family moved to Colorado so she could be coached by one of them—the legendary Italian coach Carlo Fassi.

With Carlo's guidance, Peggy became an expert at figures, which were a major part of figure skating competitions in those days and gave the sport its name. Skaters spent hours practicing figures—complicated shapes traced on the ice with the skate blade—and Peggy was one of the best at this skill. She was also known for her artistic expression in the free skate part of the competition, involving jumps and spins performed to music.

She competed at her first Olympics in 1964 and finished sixth. Four years later, at the 1968 Olympics in Grenoble, France, Peggy was the favorite for gold. She entered the competition as the three-time World champion and a five-time US champion. At the Olympics, Peggy had such a big lead after the compulsory figures portion that there was no way she would not win. Even a few mistakes in the free skate couldn't keep her from the top step of the podium.

Peggy retired from competing after winning the 1968 World Championships. She toured the US as part of the Ice Follies show and starred in TV skating specials. In 1981, she began working as a TV commentator for skating, a career that lasted almost 30 years. In 1998, Peggy was diagnosed with breast cancer and survived the disease thanks to early detection. Since then, as one of the most recognizable American skating stars, she has been an advocate for cancer screenings and early detection and a fundraiser for breast cancer charities.

Birthdate: July 27, 1948
Hometown: San Jose, California
Country Represented: USA

Olympics
Appearances: 1964, 1968
G 1968

World Championships
Appearances: 1964–68
G 1966–68
B 1965

National Championships
Appearances: 1964–68
G 1964–68

Linda Fratianne

Linda Fratianne brought glitz and glamour to figure skating, transforming skating dresses from the plain, long-sleeved dresses of her predecessors to the sequined and sparkly dresses you see on the ice today. Not only did she look good on the ice, she skated well, too. Linda won medals of every color at the World Championships during her career: gold in 1977 and 1979, silver in 1978, and bronze in 1980.

Linda first stepped onto the ice at age nine, and her mom, Virginia, noticed her natural talent right away. Within a year, Linda was working with coach Frank Carroll, then an up-and-coming coach in Southern California. He went on to become a legendary coach in the US, and Linda was his first student to compete at the Olympic Games.

In 1976, Dorothy Hamill was at the top of American skating, but Linda was not far behind. Linda was second to Dorothy at the 1976 US Championships, earning a spot on her first Olympic team at just 16 years old. She finished eighth at the 1976 Olympics in Innsbruck, Austria, and fifth at the World Championships that same year. The World Championships medals and US titles followed, and by the 1980 Olympics in Lake Placid, New York, Linda was a favorite for a medal.

Both Linda and Anett Pötzsch, from East Germany, had won World titles heading into the 1980 Olympics, and it was a close contest for gold. Linda excelled in the short and long programs—while wearing a fabulous, sparkly dress—but after the compulsory figures, she had fallen too far behind to catch up with Anett and ended up with silver.

Linda also pushed the jumping side of figure skating to grow. She was the first woman to land two different triple jumps in the same program: the triple toe loop and triple salchow. Many of Linda's competitors started doing more triple jumps to try to keep up with her, since she was able to combine jumps with artistic expression to the music.

Linda had a long career in touring ice shows, including the Ice Follies and Disney On Ice. She also coached skaters in Idaho, Colorado, and, alongside her former coach Frank Carroll, in California.

If you watch skating today, you'll see a part of Linda's legacy: a type of sit spin called a cannonball, or Fratianne spin. A sit spin is when a skater spins while crouched down on one foot with the other leg extended. Linda increased the difficulty in her Fratianne variation by grabbing her skate boot and lowering her head and shoulders towards her extended leg, showcasing impressive flexibility that skaters still emulate today.

Birthdate: August 2, 1960
Hometown: Northridge, California
Country Represented: USA

Olympics
Appearances: 1976, 1980
S 1980

World Championships
Appearances: 1976–80
G 1977, 1979 S 1978 B 1980

National Championships
Appearances: 1975–80
G 1977–80 S 1976

Amber Glenn

Amber Glenn is one to watch heading into the 2026 Olympics in Milan, Italy. The rest of the skaters in the women's field land double axels, but in the leadup to Milan, Amber was the only skater competing with a triple axel, which gives her a distinct advantage. And she mastered the jump with the persistence that has become the story of her skating career.

Amber started skating at an ice rink in a mall in Dallas, Texas, when she was five. She quickly showed promise, but the cost of ice time, coaching, skates, and costumes was difficult for her family to afford. Her dad, a police officer, worked overtime security jobs and her mom picked up extra work at the ice rink front desk. In return, Amber worked hard on the ice. To make time for training, she was homeschooled from second grade through high school.

At 14, Amber won the gold medal at the US Junior Championships, and people predicted she'd be one of skating's next big stars. But she struggled during the next season, finishing 13th in her first Nationals at the senior level. She was dealing with mental health struggles that were so serious she had to take a break from the ice. In the years before the 2022 Olympics, she worked her way back, competing at international events and winning a silver medal at the 2021 US Nationals.

At the 2022 US Championships, the final event before the Olympic team was named, Amber faced more challenges. She struggled in the short program, then tested positive for COVID-19, which took her out of the competition and off the Olympic team. She thought about retiring, but decided there was more she wanted to achieve. That included landing the triple axel she'd been practicing for years, but this time on competition ice.

To do this, Amber made some big changes to her routine. She added mental health training to help her focus and control her ADHD while competing.

The changes worked. At Skate America in October 2023, on home ice in Dallas, Amber landed the triple axel for the first time in competition. Then she got so good at it that she landed it in almost all of her programs. She won her first US Championships in 2024, 10 years after her junior title. In 2025, she won the Grand Prix Final–the first American woman to win there in 14 years–and followed that up by defending her US title. At the 2025 World Championships, she finished fifth, her highest-ever placement, and landed a triple axel in her free skate, the only one in the competition.

Through it all, Amber stays committed to taking care of her mental health. She's also the first openly LGBTQ+ woman to win the US Championships, and she hopes to inspire other skaters to be themselves and embrace their identities.

Birthdate: October 28, 1999
Hometown: Plano, Texas
Country Represented: USA

Olympics
Appearances: None–yet!

World Championships
Appearances: 2023–25

National Championships
Appearances: 2015, 2017–25
G 2024–25 S 2021 B 2023

FIGURE
#4CONTSFIG

Dorothy Hamill

Dorothy Hamill, "America's Sweetheart" of the 1970s, is just as famous for a haircut as she is for her Olympic gold medal. The 1976 Olympic champion performed in a short bob hairdo that inspired both skaters and non-skaters across the US to get haircuts just like hers.

Long before she became an icon, Dorothy was an eight-year-old girl who discovered her love of skating on a frozen pond near her house. She desperately wanted to learn how to skate backwards, so she started taking group lessons at a nearby rink called Playland. The group lessons were only one day a week, but Dorothy liked skating so much that she went to the daily public sessions to practice on her own and tried to teach herself new moves by watching other skaters. Private lessons and one-on-one coaching followed, along with summers spent at a training center in Lake Placid, New York.

Dorothy grew up admiring 1968 Olympic champion Peggy Fleming and followed in the footsteps of Janet Lynn, the 1972 Olympic bronze medalist. Dorothy finished second to Janet at the US Championships in 1973 and impressed the skating world with a fourth-place finish at the World Championships that year. After Janet retired, Dorothy took over the top spot in American skating.

She won the US Championships three times, in 1974, 1975, and 1976, and was the World silver medalist in 1974 and 1975. She also created a spin that came to be known as the Hamill Camel, a flying camel spin in combination with a sit spin. To do a flying camel, a skater jumps from one foot to the other during the spin entrance and lands to spin with their free leg stretched out behind them in an arabesque position. To create her namesake spin, Dorothy transitioned from the flying camel into a sit spin.

Heading into the 1976 Olympics in Innsbruck, Austria, 19-year-old Dorothy was competing for gold against Christine Errath of East Germany, the 1974 World Champion, and Dianne de Leeuw of the Netherlands, the 1975 World Champion. Dorothy had finished second to each of them at the last two Worlds, but at the Olympics, she was in the lead after the compulsory figures and the short program. She skated well in the free skate and earned 5.9 marks for artistic impression from all nine judges, one mark below what was then a perfect score, 6.0. The gold medal was hers.

After her Olympic win, Dorothy appeared on the cover of *Time* magazine, and the rink in her Connecticut hometown was named after her. She performed for decades in TV skating specials and in the Ice Capades and Champions on Ice shows. In 2013, she even competed as one of the celebrities on the TV show *Dancing with the Stars*.

The mother of a daughter, Dorothy is also a breast cancer survivor. In her memoir, *A Skating Life: My Story*, she shared her struggles with depression and her road to recovery in hopes of inspiring others with similar challenges.

Birthdate: July 26, 1956
Hometown: Greenwich, Connecticut
Country Represented: USA
Olympic Appearances: 1976
Olympic Medals:
G 1976
World Championship Appearances: 1972–76
World Championship Medals:
G 1976 S 1974–75
National Championship Appearances: 1971–76
National Championship Medals:
G 1974–76 S 1973
P 1972

Carol Heiss Jenkins

You can't think of Carol Heiss Jenkins without thinking of the big, bright smile that lights up her face. That winning smile was a longtime fixture in the skating world, from when she was winning gold at the Olympics, World Championships, and US Championships during her competitive career to when she was coaching at those same events decades later.

Carol grew up in New York City, one of three siblings who competed internationally in figure skating. She started skating when she was four and spent time training at the old Madison Square Garden. In 1953, when she was just 13, she competed at the US National Championships at the senior level for the first time. She finished second to Tenley Albright, igniting a rivalry that would last through the 1956 Olympics, where Albright took the gold and Carol the silver.

After 1956, it was gold all the way for Carol. She won the World Championships in 1956, beating her rival Tenley, then racked up four more consecutive victories from 1957 to 1960. To this day, Carol and Michelle Kwan are the only American women to have won five World Championship titles. Carol also won the US Championships every year from 1957 to 1960 and continued her streak by winning gold at the 1960 Olympics in Squaw Valley, California.

After the Olympics, her signature smile was on display at a ticker-tape parade through her hometown, New York City, where 250,000 fans cheered her victory.

The difficult axel jump became a signature move for Carol. Not only could she do it in either a clockwise or counterclockwise direction, a feat still rare today (skaters can typically rotate in only one direction), but she was also the first woman to land a fully rotated double axel jump. Other skaters had tried this move but failed to land fully backwards after the required two and a half rotations. And that wasn't her only first: Carol is also the first American woman to win the World Championships and the Olympics on home ice, the first woman to win back-to-back World titles, and the first woman athlete on the cover of *Sports Illustrated*.

After growing up in a skating family, Carol also married into one. Her husband is 1956 Olympic champion Hayes Alan Jenkins, and her brother-in-law is fellow 1960 Olympic champion David Jenkins. In 1976, all three of them were inducted together into the US Figure Skating Hall of Fame and the World Figure Skating Hall of Fame. Carol took a break from the ice while raising her three children. She then returned to the rink as a successful coach in the Cleveland, Ohio, area, where she taught skaters including 2002 Olympic bronze medalist Timothy Goebel and 1996 US National silver medalist Tonia Kwiatkowski.

Birthdate: January 20, 1940
Hometown: New York, New York
Country Represented: USA

Olympics
Appearances: 1956, 1960
S 1956 G 1960

World Championships
Appearances: 1953, 1955–60
S 1955 G 1956–60

National Championships
Appearances: 1953–60
G 1957–60 S 1953–56

Sonja Henie

Sonja Henie is such a legend in the sport of figure skating that her records from the 1920s and 1930s still stand today. She is the only woman to win the Olympic Games three times in a row, and is also the only 10-time World champion in the history of the sport.

Once Sonja was done competing, she had a Hollywood movie career and touring ice show empire that helped increase the popularity of skating worldwide. There has not been a star like her since.

Sonja grew up in a wealthy family in Oslo, Norway, and was an athletic kid. She did equestrian, tennis, running, skiing, and ballet before focusing on skating–where she excelled, coached by her father, a former speed skater.

Sonja competed at her first Olympics in 1924, at just 11 years old. She finished in last place, but her style was unique. While her competitors wore long skirts that reached past their knees, Sonja wore a short, fur-trimmed dress that allowed her to jump and do more athletic moves. In those days, jumps were mostly for male skaters–until Sonja started adding them to her programs. In another first for a skater, she combined her jumping skill with ballet movements inspired by her early years as a dancer. She also wore white skates instead of the traditional black, explaining that the white reminded her of the snow in her home country of Norway. Eventually, all Sonja's competitors started wearing white skates, too.

Sonja won her first World Championship title in 1927, kicking off a decade of dominance. At the next Olympics, in St. Moritz, Switzerland, in 1928, 15-year-old Sonja took the top step of the podium, having gone from last to first in just four years. She won her three Olympic titles and 10 World Championships between 1927 and 1936, after which she retired from competition to start a Hollywood career.

Sonja moved to the US, where she appeared in nine movies and starred in a touring show called Sonja Henie's Hollywood Ice Revue. Her ice show captured the hearts of audiences across North America and boosted the popularity of skating, especially in the US. On screen, she starred in films about skating, such as *One in a Million* (1936), *Thin Ice* (1937), and *Sun Valley Serenade* (1941). Sonja also loved art, and along with her husband Niels Onstad, she paid for the construction of the Henie Onstad Museum in Høvikodden, Norway, to which they donated their art collection.

Sonja's influence is still felt in women's skating today, from the short dresses to the white skates. Every skater you'll read about in this book has been influenced by Sonja in one way or another.

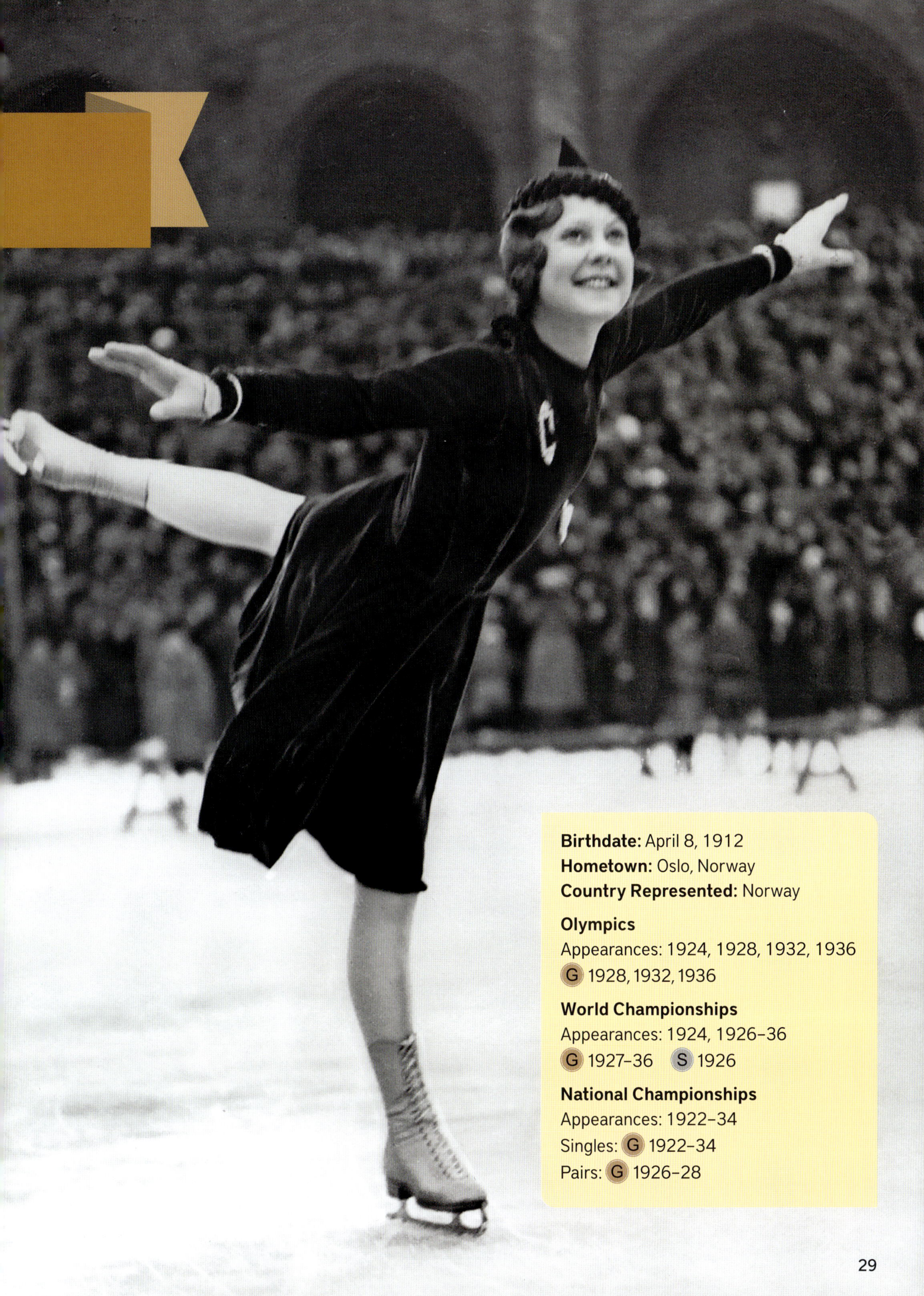

Birthdate: April 8, 1912
Hometown: Oslo, Norway
Country Represented: Norway

Olympics
Appearances: 1924, 1928, 1932, 1936
G 1928, 1932, 1936

World Championships
Appearances: 1924, 1926–36
G 1927–36 S 1926

National Championships
Appearances: 1922–34
Singles: G 1922–34
Pairs: G 1926–28

Midori Ito

Midori Ito first stepped onto the ice at age four and loved it immediately. That first day, she spotted a coach teaching another student and toddled over, saying she wanted to learn, too. The coach was Machiko Yamada, who went on to teach Midori from her earliest days on the ice all the way to the Olympics.

By age eight, Midori had landed her first triple jump. Soon, her jumping ability set her apart from other skaters. She won the All-Japan Junior Championships at age 11, then competed in her first international competition the following year.

Midori made it to her first Olympics in 1988, at 18, and landed the most triple jumps in the competition. But she finished fifth, held back by a lower placement in the figures portion of the competition. Afterward, she spent about two-thirds of her practice time on the ice working to improve her figures. Her efforts paid off at the 1989 World Championships in Paris, where she took the gold. It was the first time a skater from Japan, or any Asian country, won Worlds. Midori became a huge star at home in Japan, increasing interest in figure skating in a country where sumo wrestling and baseball were most popular.

She also got attention for pushing the technical boundaries of women's skating. She was the first woman to land a jump combination of two triple toe loops and the first to land a triple axel, which is still rare in the women's event today. She even worked on quadruple jumps, though only in practice. Midori was so good at jumping that she frequently earned perfect scores of 6.0 for her technical elements.

Midori often performed her impressive jumps close to the edge of the rink, after she'd built up enough speed to launch herself into the air. At the 1991 Worlds, she landed a jump so close to the wall that she slid off the ice, through a gap for TV cameras. She popped right back up and finished the rest of her program in time to the music, despite her brief exit from the ice.

At the 1992 Olympics, Midori fell on the triple axel in her long program but surprised everyone by trying the jump again at the end of her performance. This time, she landed it, becoming the first woman ever to do so on Olympic ice–and earning the silver medal.

After the Olympics, Midori skated in ice shows before briefly returning to competition in 1996. At the 1998 Olympics in Japan, she was chosen for the honor of lighting the Olympic torch at the opening ceremony. And Midori is still skating: At age 54, she won the gold medal in her event at the 2024 Adult International Figure Skating Competition.

Birthdate: August 13, 1969
Hometown: Nagoya, Japan
Country Represented: Japan

Olympics
Appearances: 1988, 1992
S 1992

World Championships
Appearances: 1984, 1986–91, 1996
G 1989 S 1990

National Championships
Appearances: 1984–92, 1996
G 1985–92, 1996  S 1984 B 1981

Nancy Kerrigan

Nancy Kerrigan is remembered for the grace and flexibility she showed in her trademark spiral, gliding on the ice with one leg lifted behind her while holding it at the knee, her other arm stretched out in front of her. As an Olympic figure skater, she competed in beautiful dresses created by the famous designer Vera Wang. But before she became a star, Nancy was just a kid tagging along to the neighborhood rink with her older brothers.

Her two brothers played hockey, and Nancy wanted to get on the ice, too. She started figure skating when she was six, and three years later, she was competing. Meanwhile, Nancy's parents worked hard to afford her training expenses. Her dad, Dan, was a welder who worked multiple side jobs, including driving the Zamboni (the ice-cleaning machine) at the local rink. Nancy worked just as hard on the ice, waking up at 4 AM to practice before going to school.

Her breakthrough year came in 1991, when she won bronze medals at Nationals and Worlds. She joined gold medalist Kristi Yamaguchi and silver medalist Tonya Harding in an American sweep of the World Championships that year.

Nancy's success continued at the 1992 Olympics in Albertville, France, where she once again earned a bronze medal. Then she won her first, and only, National title in 1993. The 1993 World Championships were a learning experience. Though she took the lead in the short program, Nancy struggled in the free skate and ended up in fifth place. After that, she consulted a sports psychologist to help her manage her nerves in competition.

Due to a change in the Olympic schedule, the next Winter Olympics were held again in 1994. At that year's Nationals, 24-year-old Nancy was expected to win. But she didn't even get to compete. An attacker hit her on the knee after a practice session at the rink, causing serious bruising and swelling. Nancy had to withdraw from Nationals, but she was still named to the Olympic team based on her previous achievements.

Soon, investigations revealed that one of her competitors, Tonya Harding, knew the people who had planned the attack. It seemed more like a dramatic movie plot than a figure skating rivalry, and the media attention on Nancy after the attack was intense.

Nancy worked hard to heal and get back on the ice for the 1994 Olympics in Lillehammer, Norway. She delivered a strong performance that earned her the silver medal–a remarkable recovery after being unable to skate at all just weeks earlier.

Nancy retired from competition after the Olympics to perform in ice shows and TV skating specials, many arranged by her agent, Jerry Solomon. She and Jerry got married and had three children. She also started the Nancy Kerrigan Foundation for the Visually Impaired in honor of her mother, who lost most of her vision due to a virus when Nancy was young.

Birthdate: October 13, 1969
Hometown: Stoneham, Massachusetts
Country Represented: USA

Olympics
Appearances: 1992, 1994
S 1994 B 1992

World Championships
Appearances: 1991–93
S 1992 B 1991

National Championships
Appearances: 1988–93
G 1993 S 1992
B 1991 P 1990

Yuna Kim

Yuna Kim's nickname among figure skating fans is "Queen Yuna," and she certainly is royalty in the sport, both in her home country, South Korea, and around the world.

Many of her achievements were groundbreaking for a South Korean figure skater. South Korean athletes often medaled in speed skating at the Winter Olympics, but not in figure skating—until Yuna came on the scene. When she won the Olympic gold medal in 2010, Yuna became the first figure skater from South Korea to medal at the Olympics.

And that wasn't her only first. Her bronze medal at the World Championships in 2007 was the first medal a South Korean skater ever won at that event. In fact, Yuna is the first skater from her country to medal at any international competition. She achieved this feat in 2005 on the Junior Grand Prix, a series of international competitions for the best skaters just below the Olympic level.

It all started when Yuna was six and a new ice rink opened near her home. Yuna, her parents, and her older sister went to the rink to try skating. Yuna liked it and said she wanted to keep skating, so from then on, her mother drove her to and from the rink every day. Yuna's mother was her biggest supporter throughout her skating career. In 2007, she and Yuna moved to Canada in search of more advanced coaching. There, Yuna trained six days a week, skating for two and a half hours each day and doing three hours of off-ice training, including cardio, strength training, ballet, and yoga.

Yuna often competed against Mao Asada of Japan, and the two faced off at the 2010 Olympics in Vancouver, Canada. Yuna won the gold with record-breaking scores in the short and long programs, showcasing her technical power with triple-triple jump combinations (two jumps in a row, each with three rotations in the air) and her artistic skill by connecting with the audience.

Yuna continued competing after she won the Olympics, earning a silver medal at the 2011 Worlds. She took a break during the 2012 season, explaining that it was difficult to balance her training schedule with all the interviews and opportunities that came after her Olympic win. But she returned to the ice in pursuit of a second Olympic title, winning her second World Championship in 2013 and heading into the 2014 Sochi Olympics as a favorite for the gold. She performed beautifully at the competition, but finished second to Russia's Adelina Sotnikova.

Yuna retired from competition after her second Olympics but continued performing in ice shows, including a production she created with her mother, called All That Skate. Yuna got married in 2022 and now also works as a fashion designer.

Yuna may have been the first great skater from South Korea, but she won't be the last. Her career inspired a new generation of talent in her home country, and these days, you will often see Korean skaters on the podium in international competitions.

Birthdate: September 5, 1990
Hometown: Bucheon, South Korea
Country Represented: South Korea

Olympics
Appearances: 2010, 2014
G 2010 S 2014

World Championships
Appearances: 2007–11, 2013
G 2009, 2013 S 2010–11
B 2007–8

National Cham**pionships**
Appearances: 2003–6, 2013–14
G 2003–6, 2013–14

Carolina Kostner

Carolina Kostner competed in her first World Championships in 2003, when she was 16 years old. Sixteen-year-olds at Worlds are pretty common—plenty of the greatest stars in women's figure skating won their medals in their teen years. But Carolina was still competing at the World Championships 15 years later in 2018, at the age of 31. That's pretty much unheard of in figure skating.

As skaters get older, it becomes harder to do the triple jumps that are required to win medals at the highest level of the sport. That's why a long career like Carolina's is rare. But not only could Carolina still do the triple jumps as an older skater, she also remained a fan favorite for her artistry.

With a figure-skater mom and a hockey-player dad, Carolina was on the ice by the age of four. She's actually the third Olympian in her family: Her dad played hockey for Italy in the 1984 Olympics, and her cousin skied for Italy in the 2002 Olympics. Carolina competed in both skating and skiing until age 12, when she decided to focus on skating. Two years later, her local ice rink was destroyed by a landslide, and she moved to Germany to train.

Carolina's breakthrough moment came at age 18, when she won a bronze medal at the 2005 World Championships. It was her first of six World Championship medals, including the gold in 2012. Carolina is also a five-time European champion and nine-time Italian national champion.

Throughout her long and successful career, Carolina competed in four Olympic Games. At her first Olympics, on home ice in Turin, Italy, Carolina was chosen as the Italian flag-bearer for the opening ceremony. At her third Olympics, in 2014 in Sochi, Russia, Carolina finally earned a medal, the bronze.

To compete at her fourth and final Olympics in 2018, Carolina had to make a comeback. She had been temporarily banned from competition after allegedly helping her then-boyfriend, an Olympic walking medalist, evade a required drug test. Carolina never had any drug testing violations herself and shared her commitment to drug-free sports in the aftermath of her suspension.

Her final competition was the 2018 World Championships in Milan, Italy, where she won the short program with a personal-best score. She finished the event in fourth place but still won the hearts of the Italian crowd. At the event, she reflected that when her career began, in 2003, there weren't many Italian figure skating fans, but the arena was now full of passionate supporters.

Today, Carolina skates in ice shows and coaches elite-level skaters, with a focus on the artistry that was her trademark.

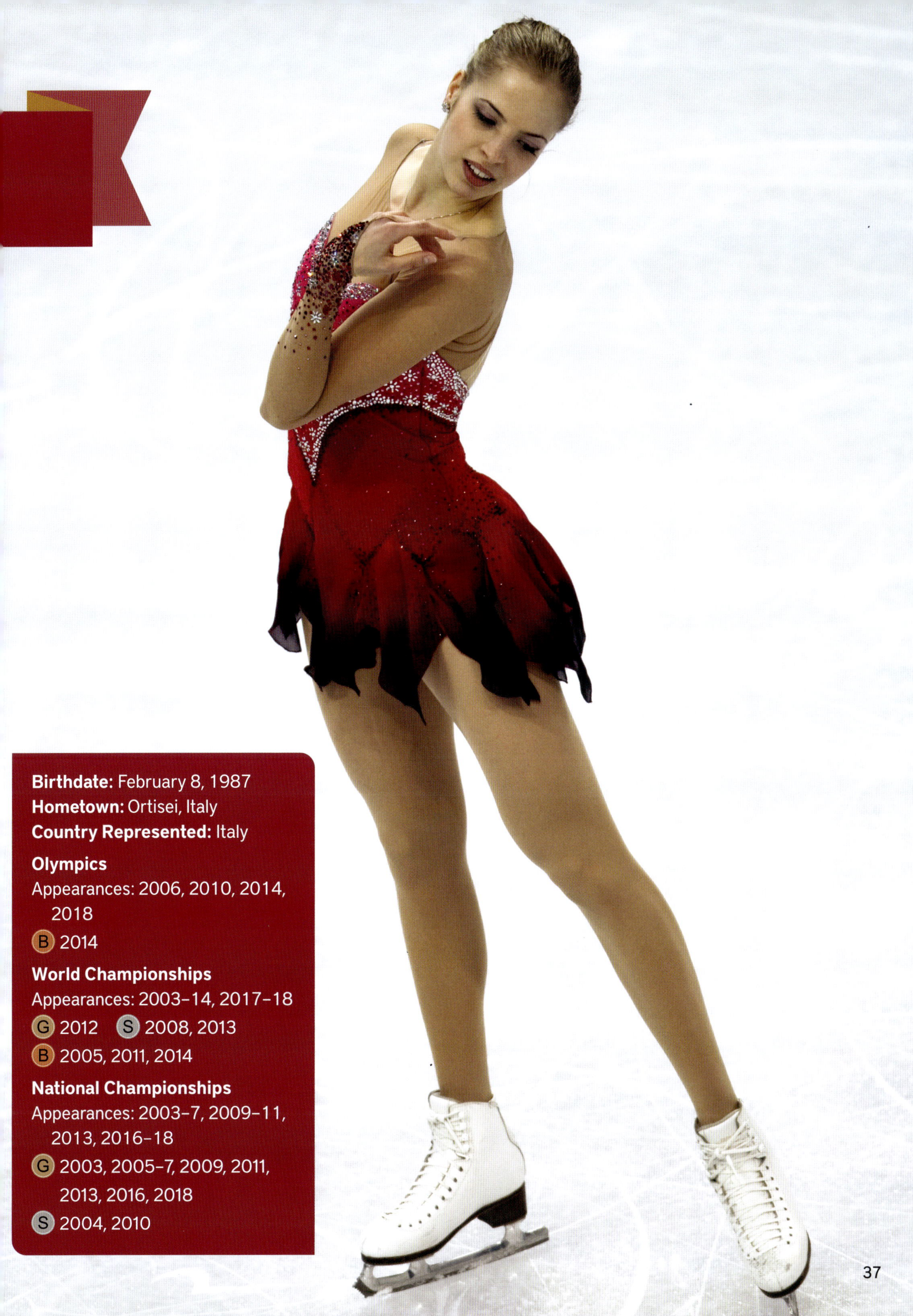

Birthdate: February 8, 1987
Hometown: Ortisei, Italy
Country Represented: Italy

Olympics
Appearances: 2006, 2010, 2014, 2018
B 2014

World Championships
Appearances: 2003–14, 2017–18
G 2012 S 2008, 2013
B 2005, 2011, 2014

National Championships
Appearances: 2003–7, 2009–11, 2013, 2016–18
G 2003, 2005–7, 2009, 2011, 2013, 2016, 2018
S 2004, 2010

Michelle Kwan

Michelle Kwan competed at the highest level of skating for 13 years. In that time, fans saw her evolve from a bright-eyed 12-year-old who finished sixth at her first US Championships into one of the greatest artistic skaters and competitors the sport has ever seen.

Michelle has won more medals than any other American skater, male or female: two at the Olympics and nine at the World Championships. She is one of only two women ever to win the US Championships nine times. The other is Maribel Vinson Owen, who coached Michelle's longtime coach, Frank Carroll, when he was competing.

Michelle started skating at age five, after watching her older brother, Ron, play hockey and her older sister, Karen, figure skate. Karen became a national-level competitive skater herself and today works as a skating choreographer. Their parents were immigrants to the US from Hong Kong and worked hard to pay for their daughters' skating lessons. For years, the girls wore used clothes, skates, and skating dresses and got up early to practice on the ice before school. When she was 11, the family made a big decision. They moved to Lake Arrowhead, a mountain town in California with a training center, so Michelle and Karen could skate more seriously. The girls' days were filled with on-ice practice, running, and weight training workouts in the gym, and they were both homeschooled.

With all that hard work, Michelle became a very consistent competitor. She remained at the top of US women's skating through four Olympic cycles. She was an alternate for the Olympic team in 1994, then a favorite for gold in both 1998 and 2002. In 2006, US Figure Skating named Michelle to the Olympic team to compete in Turin, Italy, even though she had missed the fall season with an injury. She went to Italy but withdrew from competition after suffering a new injury in practice.

Michelle was gracious in both victory and defeat throughout her career, which is part of why she is so beloved by fans around the world. A five-time World Champion, Michelle earned silver at the 1998 Olympics and bronze at the 2002 Olympics. Two of her Worlds victories came on home ice, in Minneapolis in 1998 and Washington, D.C. in 2003. At both competitions, the fans gave her a standing ovation before she had even skated.

At the height of her career, Michelle was one of the most recognizable athletes–not just figure skaters–in the world, thanks to touring ice shows, TV skating specials, and endorsements. After the 2006 Olympics, Michelle went to college and graduate school and now works in politics and diplomacy. She's worked on presidential campaigns, for the US State Department, and as the US Ambassador to Belize. She's also a mom to her daughter, Kalista.

Birthdate: July 7, 1980
Hometown: Torrance, California
Country Represented: USA

Olympics
Appearances: 1998, 2002
S 1998 B 2002

World Championships
Appearances: 1994–2005
G 1996, 1998, 2000–2001, 2003
S 1997, 1999, 2002 B 2004

National Championships
Appearances: 1993–2005
G 1996, 1998–2005
S 1994–95, 1997

Isabeau Levito

When Isabeau Levito was almost three years old, she watched the 2010 Olympic figure skating event on television. Her mom, Chiara, was a fan of the sport, and Isabeau immediately liked it, too. Mesmerized by the skaters gliding across the ice, she started imitating them in front of the TV. Soon her mom took her to the local rink, where she liked skating on the ice even more than copying the moves at home.

Fifteen years later, Isabeau is one of the favorites to make the US Olympic team in 2026. The Games will take place in her mother's hometown of Milan, Italy, where her grandmother still lives. Chiara, who moved to the US from Italy before Isabeau was born, named her daughter after a character in the movie *Ladyhawke* (1985), and she's supported Isabeau's skating career from the beginning.

Isabeau skates at a rink in Mount Laurel, New Jersey, just outside Philadelphia. She works with Yulia Kuznetsova, the same coach she started with when she was three. Back then, Isabeau loved to go fast on the ice (much like the *Ladyhawke* character, who transforms into a swift hawk!). By the time she was eight, she had mastered difficult jumps like the double axel. She switched to homeschooling when she was in fourth grade and will graduate from high school before the 2026 Olympics. After the Games, Isabeau, who loves to read, hopes to attend college.

But between now and then, she'll be focused on training. Many fans have high expectations for her Olympic performance because of all she's achieved in her career so far. After winning the gold medal at the 2022 World Junior Championships, Isabeau was on a roll. She won her first US title in 2023 and a silver medal at the World Championships in 2024.

Then, in the fall of 2024, she injured her right foot (her landing foot). She was off the ice for months and missed the 2025 US Championships. She wasn't sure if she'd be ready to compete in time for the World Championships in Boston in March 2025. But US Figure Skating named her to the World team, then cleared her to compete after evaluating her training and performance before the event. Isabeau skated two elegant, graceful programs in Boston, falling on only one jump, and finished in fourth place.

Now she has her sights set on the 2026 Olympics–and hopefully a long career after that, as well as college. She says she's inspired by her fellow Team USA skaters: Amber Glenn, who had her most successful season yet in her mid-20s, and Alysa Liu, who returned to competition after starting college at UCLA.

Birthdate: March 3, 2007
Hometown: Mount Holly, New Jersey
Country Represented: USA

Olympics
Appearances: None–yet!

World Championships
Appearances: 2023–25
S 2024

National Championships
Appearances: 2022–24
G 2023 B 2022, 2024

Tara Lipinski

Tara Lipinski is the youngest-ever Olympic champion in women's figure skating, but she actually got her start in roller skating. When she was three, her mom signed her up for roller skating because the venue was offering a free Care Bear stuffed animal for new students. Tara loved the Care Bear–and she loved roller skating, especially for an audience. When she was six, her parents wondered if she might like skating on ice instead and took her to a local rink. Tara didn't like it on her first lap around the ice, but she gave it another try, and soon, she was hooked. Skills on the ice came easily to her because she'd already mastered many of them on roller skates. Before long, she made the switch to figure skating.

Tara took lessons at a competitive training center in Delaware until her dad's job transferred him to Texas. After the family moved, they couldn't find enough ice time for Tara to practice. They decided that Tara and her mom would move back to Delaware for skating, while her dad stayed in Texas. It was a difficult choice, but it led to success for Tara.

By age 13, Tara had won a bronze medal at the 1996 US Figure Skating Championships and competed at her first World Championships. The next year, she won gold at the 1997 Grand Prix Final, the US Championships, and the World Championships. At 14, she was the youngest-ever winner of each event.

By this point, Tara had switched from regular school to a homeschool program that accommodated her practice time and competition schedule. She and her mom had moved again, to Detroit, Michigan, for training to support Tara's Olympic dreams.

Heading into the 1998 Olympics in Nagano, Japan, the women's figure skating competition was seen as a battle for gold between Tara and fellow American Michelle Kwan. Tara was the reigning World champion, but Michelle had won the 1996 World Championships and the 1998 US Championships. It was Tara who triumphed in Nagano, after a program featuring her signature triple loop-triple loop. Tara was the first woman ever to land that jump combination, which consists of two jumps in a row that take off backwards and rotate three times in the air. What makes it extra difficult–so difficult that it's still rare in competition today–is that skaters take off for the second jump on the same foot they landed on, without any toe pick assistance.

Not only is Tara the youngest-ever Olympic champion in women's figure skating, she is also the youngest individual gold medalist in Winter Olympics history. It's unlikely those records will ever be broken, since she won at age 15 and skaters now have to be at least 17 years old to compete at the Olympics.

Tara retired from competitive skating after the Olympics, then spent years touring the US with the Champions on Ice and Stars on Ice shows. She also competed in professional and made-for-TV skating events and worked as an actress. Today, she is a TV figure skating commentator and has a daughter with her husband, Todd.

Birthdate: June 10, 1982
Hometown: Sewell, New Jersey
Country Represented: USA

Olympics
Appearances: 1998
G 1998

World Championships
Appearances: 1996–97
G 1997

National Championships
Appearances: 1996–98
G 1997 S 1998 B 1996

Alysa Liu

Alysa Liu started skating because her dad was a fan of the sport. He took five-year-old Alysa to a local rink, thinking she might enjoy skating, too. And Alysa did. She loved the feeling of sliding across the ice, so her dad signed her up for learn-to-skate classes. Private lessons followed, then competitions. Her four younger siblings also tried skating, but none of them loved it as much as Alysa. By the time she was 10, Alysa was missing so much school while traveling for competitions that she switched to homeschooling. Her day began with two or three hours of practice on the ice, then schoolwork in a cubicle at her dad's law office, followed by more practice.

All that practice paid off in a series of impressive achievements at a young age. Alysa is the youngest skater ever to land a triple axel in competition, a feat she performed at age 12 in an international competition at the advanced novice level. By the time she moved up to the junior level, she was landing quadruple jumps in her programs. She is the first American woman to land a quad jump and the first woman ever to land a triple axel and quad in the same program. In 2019, she won gold at the US Championships at just 13 years old–the youngest champion ever.

Alysa defended her US title in 2020 but was still too young to compete for the US internationally. By the Olympic season in 2022, Alysa was finally old enough, at 16, to compete on the international circuit. She earned a spot at the Olympics in Beijing, China, where she finished sixth, then won a bronze medal at the World Championships. She seemed poised for even more success and a long career, but instead, she retired, wanting to experience more of life outside the ice rink.

Instead of skating, she lived a more normal teenage life: regular school and then college at UCLA. But a ski trip reminded her how much she loved feeling the breeze on her face when she was skating, and she dug out an old pair of skates and got back on the ice.

That was in January 2024. She announced her comeback in March of that year, at the not-so-old age of 18. Just one year later, in her first season back, Alysa won the gold medal at the 2025 World Championships. And she did it by focusing on fun this time around. The World Championships took place in Boston, and the home crowd erupted when Alysa took the gold. Now, after an unlikely and inspirational comeback, she is one of the favorites heading into the 2026 Olympics.

Birthdate: August 8, 2005
Hometown: Richmond, California
Country Represented: USA

Olympics
Appearances: 2022
Olympic Medals: None–yet!

World Championships
Appearances: 2022, 2025
G 2025 B 2022

National Championships
Appearances: 2019–22, 2025
G 2019–20 S 2025 P 2021

Janet Lynn

Janet Lynn is one of the greatest skaters ever, remembered more for her exuberance and freedom of movement on the ice than for any of the medals she won. She competed in the late 1960s and early 1970s, when compulsory figures made up the majority of a skater's score in competitions. Janet struggled with figures, which kept her from winning an Olympic or World title. But she was the best of her time in the free skate and performed triple jumps when it was still rare for women to do them.

Janet was so good, in fact, that the International Skating Union (ISU) changed how competitions worked. Janet competed at a time when only the free skate portion of a program was shown on TV. As a result, viewers were confused when Janet's amazing performances didn't win her first place. Usually, the winner was her rival Beatrix Schuba of Austria, who often had a huge lead after the figures. In response to the uproar from fans, the ISU added the short program to competitions in 1973, reducing the importance of figures in the final result.

If this change had happened sooner, Janet might have won more titles. But her accomplishments are still impressive. A two-time Olympian, she won bronze at the 1972 Olympics, plus silver and bronze medals at the World Championships. At home in the US, she was a five-time national champion.

Janet first took to the ice at age three, when she was living in the suburbs of Chicago. By the time she was eight, she was competing against older skaters and succeeding. Her father sold his drugstore business in Chicago so the family could move for Janet to train with a high-level coach in Rockford, Illinois. Her full name is Janet Lynn Nowicki, but she dropped her last name in competitions because it was difficult for announcers to pronounce.

With Janet Lynn as a stage name, she became a huge skating star in the US. After she retired from competition in 1973, Janet signed a $1.455 million contract with the Ice Follies touring ice show, which made her the highest-paid female athlete of her time. Fans loved watching Janet on TV, too, and her popularity helped spark the creation of the World Professional Skating Championships, for skaters who had retired from competition. She won that event in its first year, 1973, and toured with shows for two years afterward, until issues with asthma led to the end of her skating career. But the impact of her incredible free skating is still felt in the sport, where competitions no longer include compulsory figures, just a short and a long program.

Birthdate: April 6, 1953
Hometown: Rockford, Illinois
Country Represented: USA

Olympics
Appearances: 1968, 1972
B 1972

World Championships
Appearances: 1968–73
S 1973 B 1972

National Championships
Appearances: 1967–73
G 1969–73 B 1968 P 1967

Kaori Sakamoto

Kaori Sakamoto doesn't just jump on the ice, she soars. Not only are her jumps high, but she also travels across the ice as she rotates. It's a breathtaking combination that audiences around the world have enjoyed since she arrived on the senior international scene in 2018.

Kaori's jumping skill has brought her to great heights in her skating career. She is the first woman to win three straight World Championship titles since Peggy Fleming won back in 1966, 1967, and 1968.

But years before she became a champion, Kaori saw figure skating on a TV show and told her mom that she wanted to try it. Kaori was just three years old. By age eight, she was training seriously with dreams of the Olympics.

In her first full season at the senior level, 17-year-old Kaori earned a silver medal at the Japanese National Championships and a spot on Japan's 2018 Olympic team. At the Olympics in PyeongChang, South Korea, she finished sixth in the individual event and fifth in the team competition. This was only the second time the team figure skating event was part of the Olympics.

Even though she is known for her spectacular triple jumps, Kaori has also spent time working on the performance side of her skating. She's traveled to the US and Canada to work with respected choreographers and tried out different styles of skating in her programs. She has skated a short program to the soundtrack from the movie *The Matrix*, another short program to a hip-hop medley by Janet Jackson, and a long program to songs from the musical *Chicago*. Her Olympic long program in 2022 explored themes of womanhood, which was fitting for a 21-year-old who broke through a group of jump-focused Russian teenagers to earn a spot on the podium. She won the bronze medal at those Olympics, along with silver in the team event, then went on to earn her first World Championship title.

In the years that followed, Russian skaters were banned from competition because of their country's invasion of Ukraine. In their absence, and with her own prowess, Kaori dominated the women's field for the next two years, culminating in two more World titles.

It's not easy to stay at the top for long, as Kaori learned firsthand at the 2025 World Championships in Boston. In fifth place after the short program, she performed a strong free skate that earned a standing ovation, but ended up with the silver medal. She demonstrated true sportsmanship when she joyfully and enthusiastically hugged the champion, American Alysa Liu, right after Alysa's score beat Kaori's for the gold.

Heading into her third Olympic season, Kaori has her sights set on another individual medal at the 2026 Games. Win or lose, she'll be using her signature jumps and performance style along the way.

Birthdate: April 9, 2000
Hometown: Kobe, Japan
Country Represented: Japan

Olympics
Appearances: **2018, 2022**
B 2022
S (Team) 2022

World Championships
Appearances: 2019, 2021–25
World Championship Medals:
G 2022–24
S 2025

National Championships
Appearances: 2014–25
G 2019, 2022–25
S 2018, 2021

Irina Slutskaya

Irina Slutskaya is the most accomplished Russian women's figure skater ever, and she was at the top of the sport for more than a decade. She won two Olympic medals, six World Championship medals, and seven European Championships. She was the first Russian woman to win Europeans and still holds the record for most European titles won by a woman.

Throughout her long career, Irina had to overcome adversity many times. At age four, she got sick frequently, so her mom, a former skier, took her skating outside in hopes that fresh air would help. It worked. By age 10, Irina was training full-time, and five years later, she won a bronze medal at the 1994 World Junior Championships.

Irina won her first World medal, a bronze, in 1996. She finished fifth at the 1998 Olympics and won silver at the World Championships, but then had a difficult season in 1999. After a fourth-place finish at Russian Nationals, Irina was passed over for Russia's World team, despite being a two-time World medalist. That year, fellow skater Maria Butyrskaya became the first Russian woman to win the World Championships, an accomplishment many skating fans had thought would belong to Irina.

But Irina came back strong during the 1999–2000 season, winning Russian Nationals, the Grand Prix Final, and the European Championships, plus a silver at Worlds. Her first World title followed in 2002.

And that wasn't her last comeback. In 2003, she skipped the World Championships to care for her mother, who was ill. The next season, Irina herself became ill with heart problems and inflammation of the blood vessels, which made it difficult to train. She missed the 2004 Russian Nationals and finished ninth at Worlds that year. But 2005 was Irina's year: After successful medical treatment, she won Europeans for the sixth time, and Worlds for the second time.

Irina told the *New York Times* that she hopes her perseverance in the face of challenges inspires others: "Maybe somebody will watch me and say, 'My gosh, if she fought through her illness, why should I be sitting here?'"

Already a silver medalist at the 2002 Olympics in Salt Lake City, Utah, Irina earned a bronze medal at the 2006 Olympics in Turin, Italy, becoming the first, and still only, Russian woman to win a medal at two different Olympic Games.

An athletic skater, Irina also set records with her jumps. She is the first woman to land the difficult triple lutz-triple loop jump combination, in which the skater takes off backwards assisted by the toe pick, rotates three times in the air, then lands and immediately takes off from the same foot, without toe pick assistance, to rotate three times in the air once again. She is also the first to perform a Biellmann spin–in which the skater grasps their free skate blade and pulls the skate overhead and behind the back–on each foot.

After her competitive career, Irina performed in touring ice shows in the US and Russia and had three children.

Birthdate: February 9, 1979
Hometown: Moscow, Russia
Country Represented: Russia

Olympics
Appearances: 1998, 2002, 2006
S 2002 B 2006

World Championships
Appearances: 1995–98, 2000–2002, 2004–5
G 2002, 2005
S 1998, 2000–2001
B 1996

National Championships
Appearances: 1994–2003, 2005
G 2000–2002, 2005
S 1996, 2003
B 1994–95, 1997

Madge Syers

Madge Syers was a trailblazer at a time when figure skating competitions were only for men.

Born in 1881, Florence Madeline Cave, or Madge as she was known, was one of 15 children in a wealthy English family. At that time, ice skating was a social activity for the upper classes during the winter. Madge joined the local skating club in her London neighborhood, but she wasn't content just to skate socially. She wanted to compete, like the male skaters.

At the skating club, Madge met Edgar Syers, a fellow skater who also coached her. Edgar and Madge began skating together as a pairs team, and in 1899, they won the first-ever British pairs skating competition. The next year, they got married.

Madge was still determined to compete in singles skating as well as pairs. She and Edgar did some research and found that there was no rule prohibiting women from competing in the World Figure Skating Championships. It was just traditionally seen as a men's event. In 1902, the World Championships took place in London, and Madge entered the competition. When the judges found out, they wanted to ban her from participating, but without an official rule excluding women, they couldn't. Not only did Madge compete, she won a silver medal, coming in second behind the Swedish skater Ulrich Salchow (inventor of the salchow jump).

After Madge's success in 1902, the International Skating Union officially banned women from the World Figure Skating Championships. Then came several years of debate about whether women should be allowed to compete. In the meantime, Madge competed at the new British Championships, winning the first event in 1903 and the second in 1904. The event was for both men and women, and she even beat Edgar in the 1904 competition.

During this era, many women worldwide were working to gain the right to vote, and as more opportunities opened to women, so, too, did figure skating competitions. In 1906, the first women's international figure skating competition was held. It has since been recognized as the first Worlds for women, meaning that Madge's gold medal at that event–in which she beat five competitors from four countries–made her the first-ever women's World champion in figure skating.

Despite being a winter activity, figure skating was included as an event at the 1908 Summer Olympics in London. (British refrigeration technology had advanced far enough to allow for an outdoor ice surface in warm weather.) There, Madge became the first Olympic gold medalist in women's figure skating. She also competed in pairs with Edgar, and they won the bronze medal.

Madge and Edgar shared a love of the ice and also wrote books about the sport and art of figure skating. Madge died from a heart condition in 1917, at just 35 years old, after paving the way for the future of women's skating.

Birthdate: September 16, 1881
Hometown: London, England
Country Represented: Great Britain

Olympics
Appearances: **1908**
Singles: G 1908
Pairs: B 1908

World Championships
Appearances: 1902, 1906–7
G 1906–7 S 1902

National Championships
Appearances: 1903–4
G 1903–4

Debi Thomas

When Debi Thomas started figure skating at age five, few Black skaters had come before her. By the time she ended her competitive career at age 21, she had become the first Black athlete to medal at the Winter Olympics and the first Black woman to win the World Figure Skating Championships.

Debi's mom was the one who introduced her to skating. She took Debi to watch a competition, and when Debi saw the skaters performing and running around afterward with medals, she wanted to try the sport, too. She started skating at a rink in a mall, then advanced to more serious training at a rink farther away. Debi's mom drove her over 100 miles each day, between home, school, and skating practice. All the effort paid off: At age 12, Debi won the silver medal at the US Championships at the novice level.

She competed at the senior level at Nationals for the first time in 1983, at just 15 years old, finishing in 13th place. She placed sixth the next year, then, in 1985, earned silver and a trip to her first World Championships.

The year 1986 was a historic one for Debi. She won both the US Championships and the World Championships, becoming the first Black skater to win gold at each of those events. The next year, she had an Achilles tendon injury and struggled, finishing second at both the US and World Championships.

During the Olympic season in 1988, both Debi and her East German rival, 1987 World champion Katarina Witt, skated to music from the opera *Carmen*. The media coverage called the women's event the "Battle of the Carmens." Katarina won the battle, with Debi earning the bronze medal after making a few mistakes in her program. Afterward, Debi said that she had wanted to give a perfect performance and didn't fight hard enough to win after her two-footed landing on her opening jump discouraged her. (Skaters are supposed to land on one foot.) In the years that followed, she came to realize that effort was more important than perfection.

"You hate for the Olympics to have to be a learning experience, but I did learn from that," Debi said on a podcast interview in 2009.

Along with skating, education was always a priority for Debi. She was an honors student in high school and attended Stanford University full time as a pre-medicine major while competing. She took time off from school during the 1988 Olympic season, but then went back to finish her degree while performing in ice shows on the weekends. After graduating from Stanford in 1991, Debi stopped skating, went to medical school at Northwestern University, and became an orthopedic surgeon. After taking time away from medicine because of mental health struggles, Debi returned to the ice in 2023 and competed in the World Figure and Fancy Skating Championships, a competition that celebrates the art of skating.

Birthdate: March 25, 1967
Hometown: San Jose, California
Country Represented: USA

Olympics

Appearances: 1988

B 1988

World Championships

Appearances: 1985–88

World Championship Medals:

G 1986

S 1987

B 1988

National Championships

Appearances: 1983–88

G 1986, 1988

S 1985, 1987

Maribel Vinson Owen

Maribel Vinson Owen grew up in a skating family. Her grandfather was known as a skating expert around Boston, Massachusetts, and his son Thomas, Maribel's father, started skating at age four. Maribel's parents met while skating outdoors, so it's no surprise that their daughter started skating on ponds herself as a young child. Maribel loved being on the ice, just like the rest of her family.

By the time she was 16, in 1928, Maribel was one of the best figure skaters in the US. She won the first of her nine US Championships in women's singles that year and competed in her first Olympic Games. She also won a gold medal in pairs skating at the 1928 US Nationals with her first partner, Thornton Coolidge. Maribel excelled at both singles and pairs skating through hard work. She got up at 5 AM to take the streetcar from her home in Winchester, a Boston suburb, to a rink in the city. She skated before school, went back to the rink for more practice after school, then took the streetcar home.

Maribel won bronze in the women's event at the 1932 Olympics by landing an axel, the most difficult jump executed at the time. She also had a new pairs partner, George Hill, and they won four US titles together. At the 1936 Olympics, Maribel qualified in the women's event and in pairs with George, finishing fifth in both competitions.

But skating was not her only passion. Maribel also loved to write. She won her Olympic bronze medal while a full-time student at Radcliffe College, and after graduating in 1933, she got a full-time job writing for the *New York Times*. At 22, Maribel debuted as the paper's first female sportswriter, usually covering women's sports.

While making history on the page, Maribel continued making history on the ice. She practiced her figure skating at 4 AM before work. At the 1936 Olympics, she competed in two events and wrote about skiing for the *Times*. Over the course of her journalism career, she also worked for the *Boston Globe* and the Associated Press and wrote three books about skating technique.

Maribel carried her family's skating tradition into a new generation, working as a coach in the Boston area and putting her daughters, Maribel and Laurence, on the ice. "Little Maribel," as she was known, became a pairs skater, and Laurence skated in women's singles. With their mother as their coach, both won national titles of their own and competed in the 1960 Olympics. In fact, Maribel once again held multiple roles at the Olympics that year, coaching her daughters and writing for the Associated Press. Sadly, the family's skating dynasty ended in tragedy the next year, when Maribel and her daughters died in a plane crash on the way to the 1961 World Championships. The crash killed the entire US Figure Skating team. Today, the US Figure Skating Memorial Fund supports competitive skaters in memory of those who were lost.

Birthdate: October 12, 1911
Hometown: Winchester, **Massachusetts**
Country Represented: USA

Olympics
Appearances: 1928, 1932, 1936
B 1932

World Championships
Appearances: 1928, 1930–32, 1934
S 1928 B 1930

National Championships
Appearances: 1926–33, 1935–37
Singles:
G 1928–33, 1935–37
S 1927 B 1926
Pairs:
G 1928–29, 1933, 1935–37
S 1930–32

Katarina Witt

When Katarina Witt won her first competition at the age of seven, the prize was a stuffed animal. When she won the Olympic Games, the prize was not only a gold medal but also freedom to leave her repressive home country of East Germany. Skating was her ticket to a better life.

Katarina was born in 1965 and raised in Karl-Marx-Stadt, East Germany (now Chemnitz, Germany). She started skating when she was five years old, and her talent soon stood out, earning her a spot at a state-run sports school. There, she spent years training intensely with older skaters, including 1980 Olympic champion Anett Pötzsch, who later married Katarina's brother. In addition to their on-ice practice, skaters at the school spent hours training in ballet and soccer.

After Anett, Katarina was the next great German figure skating star. She became a four-time World champion, six-time European champion, and a two-time Olympic champion. She was also the first woman to land a triple flip jump in competition.

Katarina captivated audiences with her performance quality and intimidated competitors with her mental toughness. She was consistent in competition and thrived under pressure. At the 1987 World Championships in Cincinnati, Ohio, she had to compete after great performances by two Americans, Debi Thomas and Caryn Kadavy. Katarina needed to skate better than both of them, and she did, winning the title.

Katarina beat another American, Rosalynn Sumners, for gold at the 1984 Olympics, and defended her title at the 1988 Olympics. In the process, she became only the second woman skater to win back-to-back Olympic gold medals, after three-time Olympic champion Sonja Henie of Norway.

The '88 Olympics are remembered for the "Battle of the Carmens" in the women's event, as both Katarina and her rival Debi Thomas chose music from the opera *Carmen* for their free skate. Debi made mistakes in her *Carmen* program, and the judges preferred Katarina's theatrical interpretation of the music, giving her the gold.

After her Olympic triumphs, Katarina had permission from her government to skate professionally in touring ice shows in the US. This was a rare opportunity–her parents were not even allowed to leave East Germany to watch her skate in the Olympics.

In 1994, a special change in the Olympic rules allowed professional athletes to compete alongside amateurs. Katarina, ever the intense competitor, returned to Olympic ice in Lillehammer, Norway, and finished in seventh place. This time she represented a reunified, democratic Germany, and her parents were able to travel outside the country to watch her skate.

In 2008, she performed in a farewell tour ice show in Germany, officially ending her performing career, but her involvement with skating continues. She started a production company in Germany for ice shows and TV specials, works as a TV commentator for figure skating in Germany and the US, and also has a foundation to help children with disabilities.

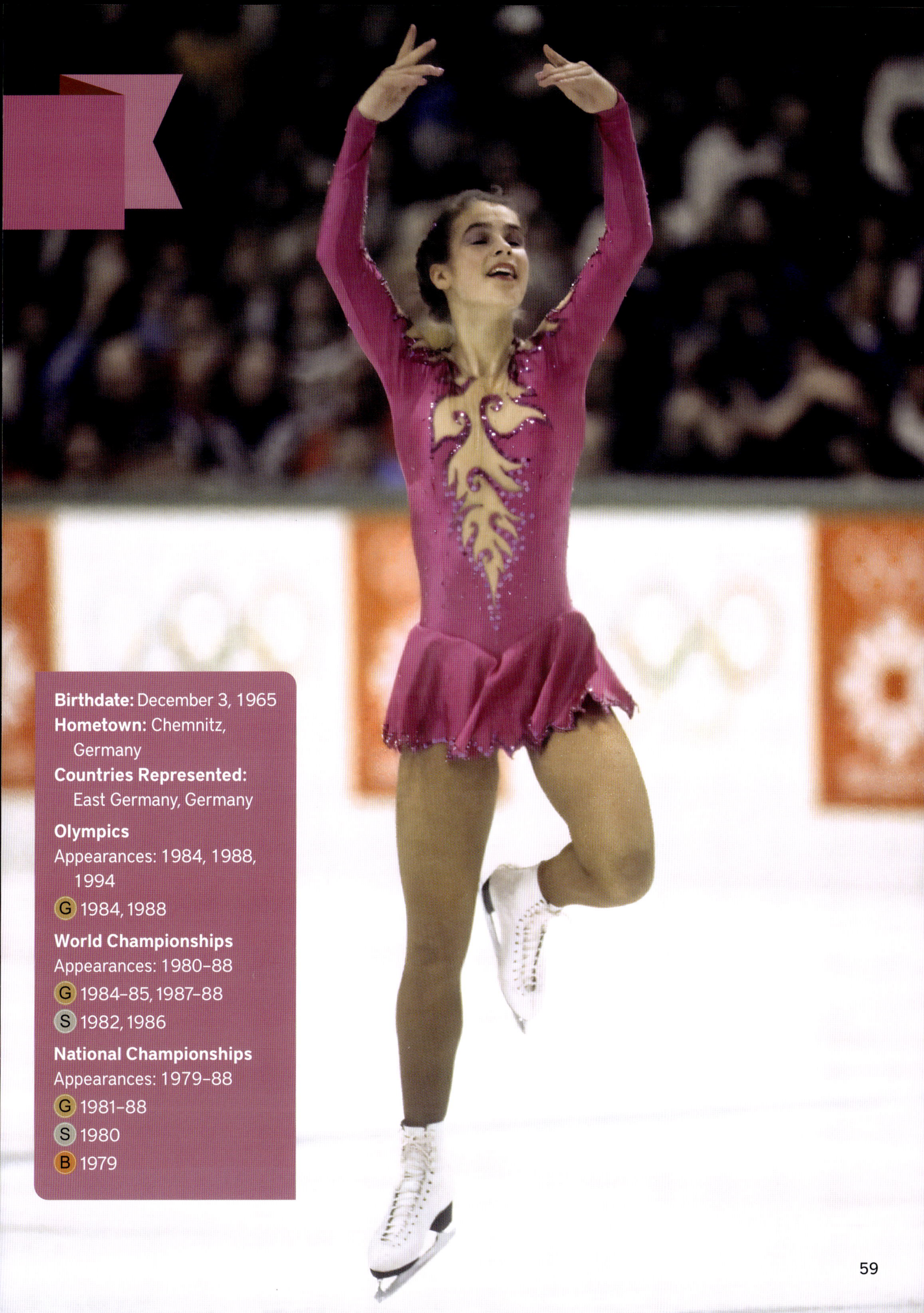

Birthdate: December 3, 1965
Hometown: Chemnitz, Germany
Countries Represented: East Germany, Germany

Olympics
Appearances: 1984, 1988, 1994
G 1984, 1988

World Championships
Appearances: 1980–88
G 1984–85, 1987–88
S 1982, 1986

National Championships
Appearances: 1979–88
G 1981–88
S 1980
B 1979

Kristi Yamaguchi

Kristi Yamaguchi was such a talented, hardworking skater that she won national and international medals in both women's and pairs skating. But to reach her ultimate dream of Olympic gold, she had to make a choice and decided to focus on her singles career. It all paid off when she won gold at the 1992 Olympics.

It was a long way from her first steps on the ice as part of a physical therapy routine. Kristi was born with clubfoot, a condition where the feet are turned inward and pointed downward, and she spent much of her early years in casts and corrective shoes. Her older sister Lori was already a skater, and doctors thought the sport could help strengthen Kristi's feet and legs, so at age six, Kristi took to the ice.

Soon she was competing in women's singles and in pairs skating with her partner, Rudy Galindo. She juggled both events at competitions for seven years of her career. During that time, she and Rudy won the World Junior Championships and two US National Championships at the senior level. When they won Junior Worlds in 1988, Kristi also took the gold in the women's event, making her the first woman to win gold in two different events at the same World Junior Championships. It's a major accomplishment to win one gold medal at Junior Worlds, let alone two, so the feat is a testament to Kristi's talent. No one has done it since.

Despite this twofold success, Kristi decided to stop pairs skating in 1990. Her coach moved to Canada and Kristi followed, while Rudy stayed in California. The distance made the partnership too challenging to maintain. With her focus on only one event, Kristi won the World Championships in 1991, then her first US title in 1992. Armed with a difficult triple lutz-triple toe loop combination, she went on to win Olympic gold and a second World Championship title.

Kristi's Olympic victory was the first for an American woman skater since 1976, when her childhood idol Dorothy Hamill won. Kristi went on to a successful career with touring ice shows, much like Dorothy. She toured with Stars on Ice from 1992 to 2002 and also participated in professional competitions and made-for-TV skating shows.

Off the ice, she created the Always Dream Foundation, which supports literacy for children and families, and became a children's book author. Kristi and her husband, former NFL player Bret Hedican, met at the 1992 Olympics and have two daughters. One of her daughters took up figure skating, too, coached by Kristi's former pairs partner, Rudy.

In 2008, Kristi won another championship—this time in the ballroom on the TV show *Dancing with the Stars*. She is a member of the US Figure Skating Hall of Fame and the World Figure Skating Hall of Fame.

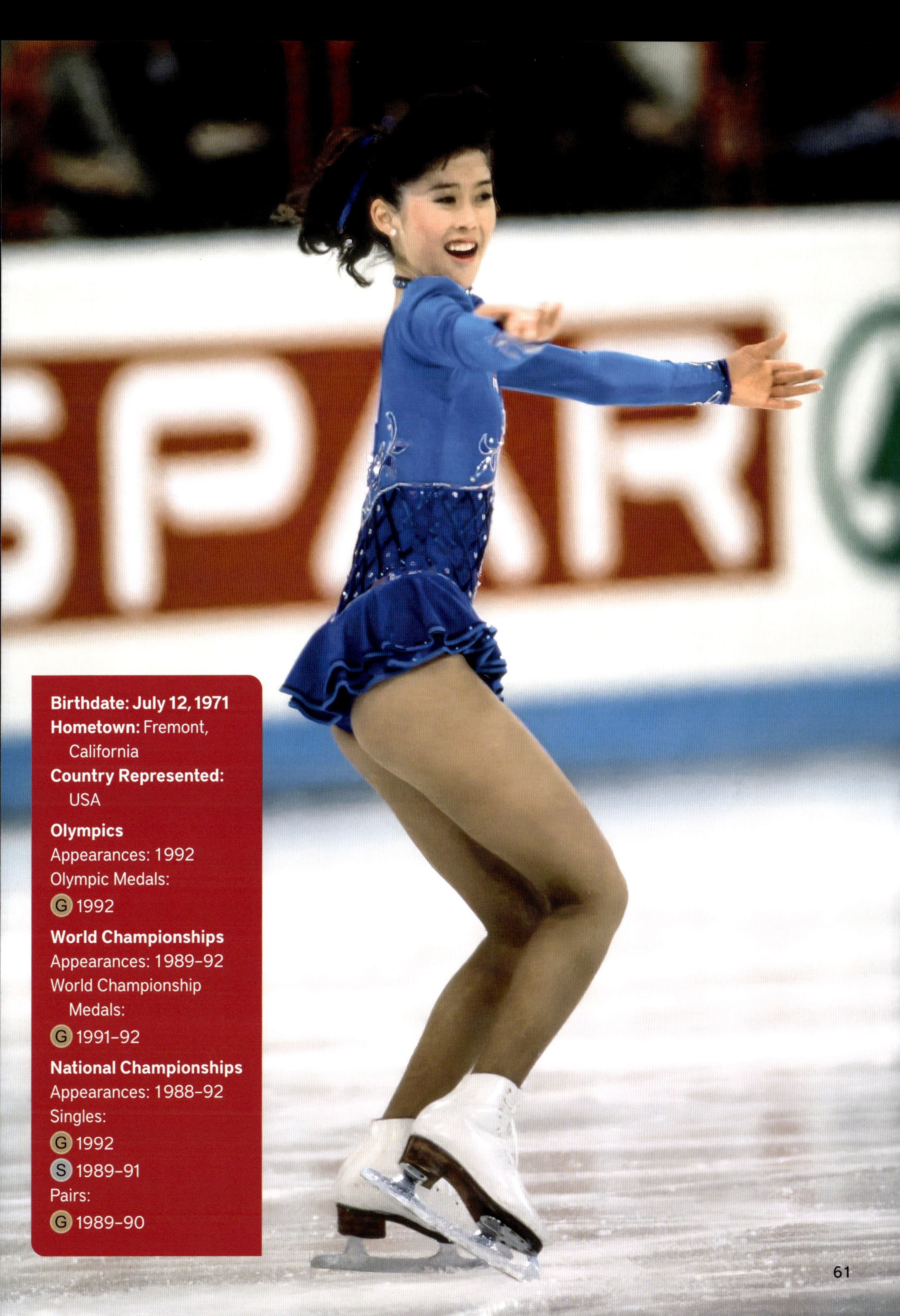

Birthdate: July 12, 1971
Hometown: Fremont, California
Country Represented: USA

Olympics
Appearances: 1992
Olympic Medals:
G 1992

World Championships
Appearances: 1989–92
World Championship Medals:
G 1991–92

National Championships
Appearances: 1988–92
Singles:
G 1992
S 1989–91
Pairs:
G 1989–90

Skating Terms Glossary

axel: The most difficult of the six figure-skating jumps, and the only one with a forward takeoff. It requires an extra half revolution for a backward landing, so a single axel rotates one and a half times, a double axel two and a half times, and a triple axel three and a half times. The jump was named for its inventor, Norwegian skater Axel Paulsen, who did the first axel in the late 1800s.

camel spin: A spin performed with the skater's leg stretched behind and the foot at hip level.

compulsory figures: Complicated shapes traced on the ice with the skate blade. Figures gave the sport of "figure skating" its name. They counted for the majority of a skater's final score until 1973, then were eliminated from competitions entirely in 1990.

edges: Skate blades have two edges: an inside and an outside. Skaters use their edges by leaning into a curve and bending both their knees and ankles. Outside edges lean outside the body, towards the pinky toes, and inside edges lean inside towards the big toe. Edges help skaters create speed and turn, and jumps are identified by which edge is used on the takeoff.

European Championships: A competition held annually for skaters on the continent of Europe.

Four Continents Championships: A competition held annually for skaters from the Americas, Asia, Africa, and Oceania.

flip: A jump (not a backflip!) that takes off from a backward inside edge, with the toe pick used to vault the skater into the air.

Grand Prix: A series of international competitions culminating in a final competition, the Grand Prix Final.

jump combination: When a skater performs multiple jumps in a row, without any steps in between.

junior level: The level of competition just below senior (Olympic) level.

long program: The second part of a skating competition, a longer routine also called the free skate (because the requirements are looser and there can be more variety in the jumps and spins performed).

loop: A jump where the skater takes off backwards, with the outside leg in front, using the curve of the outside edge on the back leg to push up into the air.

lutz: A jump that takes off from a backward outside edge, with the toe pick used to vault the skater into the air. Named for Austrian skater Alois Lutz, who did the first lutz in the early 1900s.

Nationals: A shorthand reference to the US Figure Skating Championships.

novice level: The level of competition for younger elite skaters, two levels below senior (Olympic) level.

pewter medal: Medal for a fourth-place finish at the US Championships.

revolution: A turn in the air during a skating jump. Jumps are categorized by the number of revolutions they require:

- *double:* A jump that rotates twice in the air.
- *triple:* A jump that rotates three times in the air.
- *quad:* A jump that rotates four times in the air.

salchow: A jump named after its inventor, Ulrich Salchow of Sweden. The skater takes off backwards, off an inside edge, without any assistance from the toe pick.

senior level: The Olympic level of competition, the highest level at which a skater can compete.

short program: The first part of a skating competition, a shorter routine with required jumps and spins.

sit spin: A spin performed in a squat position with one leg straight in front.

toe loop: A jump that starts on the back outside edge of the front foot, using the toe pick of the back foot to vault the skater into the air as the front foot slides past it on the takeoff.

toe pick: The sharp, pointed part at the front of a skate blade, used in some jumps to help a skater leap into the air.

Worlds: A shorthand reference to the World Figure Skating Championships.